SPIDER
ON THE
FLOOR

Raffi Songs to Read®

SPIDER ON THE FLOOR

Words and music by Bill Russell

Illustrated by Truc Kelley

Troll Associates

Published by Crown Publishers, Inc., a Random House company,
201 East 50th Street, New York, New York 10022

CROWN is a trademark of Crown Publishers, Inc. RAFFI SONGS TO READ and SONGS TO READ are registered trademarks of Troubadour Learning, a division of Troubadour Records Ltd.

Manufactured in the United States of America

Library of Congress Cataloging-in-Publication Data
Raffi.
  Spider on the floor / illustrated by True Kelley.
    p.   cm. — (Raffi songs to read)
  Summary: Presents the illustrated text to the song about the curious spider. Includes musical notation.
  1. Children's songs—Texts.   [1. Spiders—Songs and music.
2. Songs.]   I. Kelley, True, ill.   II. Title.   III. Series: Raffi.
Raffi songs to read.
PZ8.3.R124Sp 1993
782.42164' 0268—dc20   92-33442
ISBN 0-517- 59381-5 (trade)
      0-517- 59464-1 (lib. bdg.)

10 9 8 7 6 5 4 3 2 1   FIRST EDITION

Printed in the United States of America, bound in Mexico.

Front cover photograph © David Street
Back cover photograph © Patrick Harbron

There's a spider on the floor, on the floor.

There's a spider on the floor, on the floor.
Who could ask for any more
than a spider on the floor?
There's a spider on the floor, on the floor.

Now the spider's on my leg, on my leg.
Oh, the spider's on my leg, on my leg.

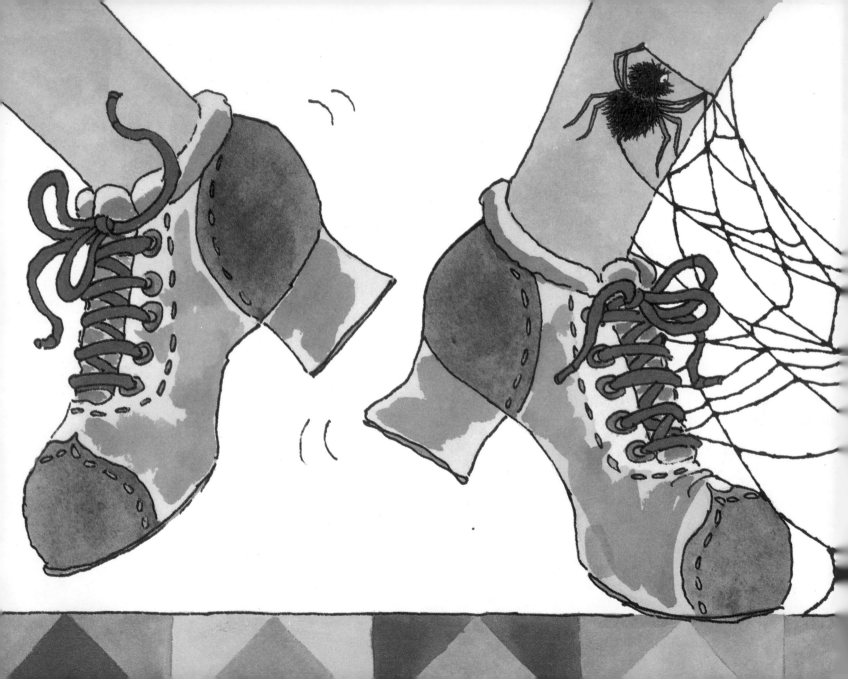

Oh, he's really big! This old spider on my leg.
There's a spider on my leg, on my leg.

Now the spider's on my stomach, on my stomach.
Oh, the spider's on my stomach, on my stomach.

Oh, he's just a dumb old lummock,

this old spider on my stomach.
There's a spider on my stomach, on my stomach.

Now the spider's on my neck, on my neck.
Oh, the spider's on my neck, on my neck.

Oh, I'm gonna be a wreck,

I've got a spider on my neck.
There's a spider on my neck, on my neck.

Now the spider's on my face, on my face.
Oh, the spider's on my face, on my face.

Oh, what a big disgrace,
I've got a spider on my face.
There's a spider on my face, on my face.

Now the spider's on my head, on my head.
Oh, the spider's on my head, on my head.

Oh, I wish that I were dead,
I've got a spider on my head.
There's a spider on my head, on my head.

There's a spider on the floor, on the floor.
There's a spider on the floor, on the floor.
Who could ask for any more
than a spider on the floor?

There's a spider on the floor, on the floor. . .

Spider on the Floor

Words and music by Bill Russell

Modulate up a semitone with each verse for six verses.
Spoken phrase after verse 6. Verse 7 in original key.

1. There's a spi-der on the floor, on the floor. There's a spi-der on the floor, on the floor. Who could ask for an-y more than a spi-der on the floor? There's a spi—der on the floor, on the floor. 2. Now the floor.

2. Now the spider's on my leg, on my leg.
   Oh, the spider's on my leg, on my leg.
   Oh, he's really big! This old spider on my leg.
   There's a spider on my leg, on my leg.

3. Now the spider's on my stomach, on my stomach.
   Oh, the spider's on my stomach, on my stomach.
   Oh, he's just a dumb old lummock, this old spider on my stomach.
   There's a spider on my stomach, on my stomach.

4. Now the spider's on my neck, on my neck.
   Oh, the spider's on my neck, on my neck.
   Oh, I'm gonna be a wreck, I've got a spider on my neck.
   There's a spider on my neck, on my neck.

5. Now the spider's on my face, on my face.
   Oh, the spider's on my face, on my face.
   Oh, what a big disgrace, I've got a spider on my face.
   There's a spider on my face, on my face.

6. Now the spider's on my head, on my head.
   Oh, the spider's on my head, on my head,
   Oh, I wish that I were dead, I've got a spider on my head.
   There's a spider on my head, on my head.

Spoken: But he jumps off...

7. *Repeat 1st Verse*